Critical Process Writing

Brett Elizabeth Blake

This book is part of the *Writing Critically* Series

Series Editor: Brett Elizabeth Blake

ISBN 978-1-64504- (Hardback)
ISBN 978-1-64504- (Paperback)
ISBN 978-1-64504-(E-Book)

Library of Congress Control Number: 2020937661

Printed on acid-free paper

Copyright © 2020 DIO Press Inc, New York
https://www.diopress.com

For all the "Roberts" in my life: My late father, Robert W. Sr., who taught me so much about writing and the importance of listening to, and including, the many voices of all our students; I miss you terribly. Robert W. Blake, Jr., who continues to be a wonderful brother, friend, confidant, and academic extraordinaire; and of course to my son, Robert "Robbie" Clark Moe, who has always been my joy and my raison d'être. In the words of the Scottish poet and writer, Robbie Burns, "Dare to be honest and fear no labor!" "Ae fond kiss to you all!"

TABLE of CONTENTS

WHAT IS A CRITICAL APPROACH TO PROCESS WRITING?

Untitled
My heart breaks for the girl
The one who is scared inside
For the girl whose doubts
Who questions herself more often than not
Imagine what she would do
If she knew just how fierce she was
Oh she'd take over the world
And the hearts she would break
If she knew that she had what it takes

Nathonya, a graduate student in a class I teach entitled, "Teaching Writing", found that not only did the *process* of writing allow her to "speak" in ways she had not/could not have before, but it also helped her to understand how important it would be in her (soon-to-be elementary) classroom in New York City to allow for all voices to be heard in a safe space. She also saw that the *product* she created was different than the scripted essays she had written most of her life, and yet she struggled with knowing she would have to instruct her students to follow such scripts if they were to become "successful" in schooling in contemporary America in 2020.

It is through her eyes and others like her that it had become apparent to many of us in the field of education that classroom writing had been re-relegated to the standardized, codified, devoid-of-voice writing we remember as we look back to the history of writing through the last century in American schools. Indeed, it is precisely through a review of the history of the field that we can follow its trajectory to a return to what I call this, "re-relegation"—a crucial moment in time where our schools, communities, and societies are once again making pointed efforts to drown out the voices of the voiceless.

From simply putting words onto paper in the 1890s to a push for penmanship at the turn of the twentieth century, to a focus on grammar and spelling (grounded in behaviorist theory) in the 1950s, to the 1970s and 1980s where groundbreaking classroom-based research (Ayers, 1993; Blake, 1980; Elbow, 1973; Graves, 1983 and Murray, 1968) refocused efforts on classrooms themselves, where successful models of process writing (and learning in general) began to highlight how commonplace it was for students to become motivated to write more and to develop a greater sense of collaboration and community at virtually all grade levels (with grammar, spelling, and syntax being attended to last) (Calkins, 1986; Graves, 1983). Writing was no longer seen as a linear process whereby students could be taught by memorizing formulaic steps to learn to write, but rather it was hailed for its recursive nature as students were encouraged to move among and within the five stages of process writing: brainstorming, drafting, revising, editing, and publishing. Indeed, according to Murray (1968), the old-school notion of "dissecting" writing hurt students' abilities to write, while both Elbow (1981) and Murray (1968) highlighted how writing was not a "solitary" act, but was best produced "collaboratively" where writers discovered meaning, not the other way around.

Indeed, according to Blake (1980), it was crucial that all writers understand just what it is "real writers" did when composing:

> Why do you need to understand the composing process? Many textbooks on writing state that to write, you must first make a detailed outline, find out exactly and completely what you want to say and simply write out what you know. However, experienced writers will tell you this isn't at all what they do. John Updike put it this way: "[W]riting and re-writing are a constant search for what one is saying", and Peter Elbow (1976) reminds us, "The common-sense, conventional understanding is as follows: Writing is a two-step process. First, you figure out your meaning, then you put it into language… Meaning is not what you start out with but what you end up with."

And yet now, writing has once again been relegated to a series of lock-step directions suited (and designed for) students taking state-wide exams that would prepare them to be "career- and college-ready", thus awakening educators to the notion that there could not be a more propitious time for a book on "critical process writing." Like in the 1960s, educational systems around the world now find themselves (driven often by countries' political populist movements) mired deeply in the scourge of racism, poverty, segregation, and fear and loathing of immigrants and refugees and the resultant inequities of schooling (as seen in the U.S.'s accountability movements such as The No Child Left Behind Act, Race to the Top; and The New Common Core Standards, [NCSS]—a movement began by a group of business leaders to direct what is taught in our schools, how it is taught, and how to decide how this so-called knowledge is measured). A return to a scripted "behavioral objectives" model is being touted, and a revival of basic skills (especially for those of immigrant backgrounds and/or of color) are being packaged as the only way to get "those" children to learn. This is most apparent in our writing classrooms where an emphasis on formulaic expository and persuasive writing (recommended to consume more than 70% of students' writing by the time they reach high school in all subjects, including math and science) undergirds our schools' focus on the scientific/mathematical way of knowing, above all others. In recent years, this emphasis left a strange silence about the current and future state of process writing in the classroom.

What is critical process writing?

Critical writing, or a critical approach to process writing, is grounded on the ideas of the early scholars of a process approach, as discussed above. But it goes further, resting firmly on the notion that the implementation of process writing in the classroom should "... reflect more than just a desire [by the teacher] to foster an individual's story" (Willinsky, 1990). Instead, it should "represent a common, critical project in the social dimensions of literature and voice that begins with the student's own situation" (p. 55). A critical approach to process writing (as enacted through a writers' workshop) becomes, then:

> A literacy enfranchisement through a sort of collective sensibility and strength...[and through] a shared commitment and co-operative nature of the process (Willinsky, p. 45).

Literacy as it often has been traditionally defined, is "sanctioned," framed from within "particular textual interpretative processes currently being canonized" that "disguise[s] cultural and ideological assumptions and perceptions" (Kell, 1997, p 242). Literacy, under this definition, excludes large numbers of students from participating in "schooled" literacy events whose cultural and ideological assumptions are everything in what they write and whose assumptions may be very different from white, middle-class students. As literacy practices are being canonized around the world, these practices are being challenged as "cultural artifacts" that seek to disguise, hide and silence crucial cultural and ideological assumptions. Regarded as dangerously value-laden, encoded, and "saturated" with social and political purposes, these canonized literacy practices are inextricably linked to power, becoming, in effect, a major vehicle for "identifying, manipulating, and changing power relations between people" (Hornberger & Skilton-Sylvester, 1998, p. 28).

In poor communities, in refugee camps, in immigrant enclaves, where students are racialized and speak other dialects and/or languages, schooled literacy simply does not "articulate with the existing literacy practices in the community "(Kell, 1997, p. 249), and so by its very nature, schooled literacy cannot, and does not, give voice to the less powerful.

Voice is an elusive, complex, and controversial concept. To researchers of writing in classrooms (Atwell, 1987; Blake, 1997; Calkins, 1983, 1986; Graves, 1983; Murray, 1968), voice is central to the process of writing itself. Expressing one's voice becomes the primary avenue in achieving ownership and control of one's writing, while at the same time, students are given opportunities to learn the value and purpose and peer review and collaboration, shared knowledge, and community. Other writing theorists (Bakhtin, 1981, 1986; Dyson, 1993; Gilbert, 1981; Lensmire, 1993, 1994) have addressed how and why a process approach to writing—what I would term a "critical" approach—becomes the site for significant tension and struggle over issues like ownership and voice. It can be through a close and detailed study of students' voices that we can begin, once again, to move toward a more positive yet critical analysis of the struggles of all students, leading us toward curricular and attitudinal changes.

The *products* that writers produce are as centrally important as the *process* writers undertook to get there, especially among students that have traditionally struggled to be heard. Here, in what I have termed the "cultural texts" (Blake, 1995) that writers produce—those that help us (and them) to explore what the writer has produced—for example, how these finished products helped students (or have shown us as educators) the how, why, when, and where these texts illustrate or perpetuate versions of gender, race, class, worth, country of origin, and global citizenship. All writing is sociohistorical and it is the *products* of the writers that convey their realities—realities often different from the so-called status quo.

As educators, we can provide opportunities for the inclusion of students' diverse lived experiences and voices in our curricula. In fact, according to Bigelow (1990), it may be our moral responsibility to help students discover that their "lives are important sources of learning" as we push them to "use their stories as windows not only on their lives, but on society [as a whole]" (p. 439). Indeed, in the words of Kincheloe (2008), teaching resides as much in the heart as in the mind, and that (among other qualities), teachers need to, "be concerned with the 'margins' of society, the experiences and needs of individuals faced with oppression and subjugation" (in Blake, 2016, pg. 124). This seems to be most apparent in our writing classrooms and other sites where writing can be used to express and support those voices of the voiceless.

Organization of the book

Grounded in a process approach to writing, a "critical" approach, also follows five recursive steps: brainstorming, drafting, revising, editing and publishing. It also heavily emphasizes the inherently collaborative nature of writing by the inclusion always of at least one peer conference (see Appendix A for a simple peer conferencing sheet any writer can use; one that can be adapted, shortened, lengthened, and/or focused on a particular genre).

Each of the following five chapters explains and describes a separate genre (personal, narrative, poetry, expository, and persuasive) and includes student samples from students in elementary school to graduate school, especially from those who felt they had never been "heard" before. For example, I share one student's writing, a refugee with whom I worked in the camps of Paris, who had walked with his cousin across Africa, was jailed in Libya, arrived in Italy, then hitchhiked to Paris—his country of origin was a former French colony). All examples are presented in their original unedited versions with grammar, spelling, and syntactical errors intact. Each has been chosen to highlight a student's voice that may not have initially felt comfortable or worthy enough to write about and/or share their writing. This refugee student exudes this most poignantly.

CHAPTER TWO

CRITICAL PERSONAL WRITING

Everyone does personal writing in some form or another: they record their experiences in a diary or online in a blog, they write and exchange emails, they write letters to editors of newspapers or their Congresswoman, and they may even (still) write vacation postcards to family and friends (like a good friend, Lenny, is passionate about). Personally, writing is usually informal and is usually intended for a trusted, known audience. Often, in classrooms, personal writing takes place as "journaling".

In most schools in the United States, personal journal writing extends beyond the early grades to include using personal and/or response journals (where the student can ask a question in a safe space and the teacher replies in his or her journal), or in secondary classrooms to respond to a math problem or a historical event—for example, as students often tie in their own experiences to help make connections to a difficult concept.

Below, I highlight the struggle of a fifth-grade student and English language learner who had just finished reading the book, *The World War II at Monte Cassino*, (widely known as one of the toughest and bloodiest battles of World War II; alternatively called The Battle for Rome). And yet, even after the teacher reviewed the book for the class, highlighting some of the important facts behind this strategic and crucial battle, this student struggled with making sense (or even caring to make sense of) the book's content or importance. Trying to help the student understand what he had read, the teacher then directed him to use his social studies response journal to try to connect the book to his personal life in any way and/or to "privately" document the student's struggle with the material, and/or why he was so re-luctant to even try to understand the content. Here is the student's journal entry:

Journal Comment.

The world war II at Monte Cassino

Dear Teacher,

When Larry was in the

Army he had to eat

Army food and he

Said it tasted alful

And he didn't like

It. When my dad was in the army he had to eat army

Too. And he didn't like it either.

What I like about this book is

That it reminds me of my dad

That's the only

Thing I like

About this book. Well I

Think I'm done talking

About this

Book.

Sincerely,

Indeed, research shows that in the past few decades, journal writing has been shown to not only help students to understand concepts more deeply as they improve their writing, but can also help students explore their own cultural identities as they grow and learn in an increasingly globalized world. This may be especially crucial among students who are English learning and/or come from cultures where personal writing is not necessarily valued. As Sharma (in Blake & Maslak, 2019) describes:

> Reading and thinking have no use; plowing your field will bring you food, said most farmers to their children in a little village…in India… where my family had migrated from Nepal. I always recognized learning to read and write as the absolute means for personally escaping poverty…and eventually being connected again with those once-isolated communities. I first learned to read and write in English and [it was then] that I first seriously thought about the role of literacy in broader, societal terms (Sharma, pg. 53).

In the twenty-first century, the sign of an educated person, throughout the Western World and in Asian countries like China and Japan, indeed, remains one who can connect the power of the written word to the world itself.

Academically, then, personal journal writing affords students opportunities to not only gain a deeper understanding of a subject matter, but to also ask "private" questions to the teacher on a particular concept needed to complete a particular assignment or project like a science lab, for example. Like the middle-school student (above), personal journal writing can also help students make critical connections to the subject at hand to one's personal life, helping him, for example, to perhaps not only deepen his understanding of World War II (the event) but also of his own cultural self through a family member's experience (his and family's identity). With extended practice in journal writing, I have seen students develop a higher level of writing in their English Language Arts classroom and across disciplines in their content area classrooms.

However, getting students to begin any type of writing is not easy, especially if they are English language learners, struggling learners, or simply students who have always been told their writ-

Chapter Two

ing was terrible (as witnessed by red pen marks and scribblings covering their pieces, usually only focusing on grammar and spelling).

One of the most enduring "starts" for various kinds of writing (including poetry and narrative (which I will discuss and make connections throughout the next 2 following chapters) is that of an "early memory" or "memoir" writing. The major reason for this rests on the assumption that everyone has a story to tell, especially about themselves. Below is a "script" of prompts I have successfully used with all types of students, including undergraduates and graduates, both at the master's and doctoral level. It has even helped incarcerated students find their voice as they put pen to paper (Blake, 2004), believing in themselves again as they told stories of their lives. Here is a sample of a secondary student writing about a painful time in her past as a little girl. I also include here the general task and prompts, created for the most reluctant of writers:

My Earliest Memory

I had been asleep. Someone—my father, I suppose—snapped on the wall switch. I sat up in bed, surprised and confused by the blinding light. I sensed that the loud noise in my dream had been the door knob that had been crashed against the bedroom wall. People were shouting outside in the hallway. A woman was crying. I think I was not aware, then, that there were anger and hate in those sounds. There was only my fear in that room. It was a smothering fear that I didn't want to take in. I remember that I held my breath and shut my eyes as tightly as I could. I crawled deep down inside myself into a little black hole where no one could reach me. But my father shook me and made me look at a suitcase. He asked me if I wanted him to go away. And I answered from that walled in place that I wanted him to stay. He left the room, then. I took my fear down under the blankets and curled up with it. Nothing more got in.

When I was a grown woman with children of my own, I finally asked my mother about that night. She didn't remember it. But I have never forgotten it—nor the realization that I had lied to my father.

Task:

Our childhood memories remain with us for all of our lives. Sometimes our first memories are sad, sometimes happy. In many cases, when we think back to our own childhood, we are amazed at how vividly some memories stand out in our minds. Now, you can write abut the earliest time you can remember as a child, a time when you were either terribly frightened or enormously happy. Try to step back now and let the child who you were—but is no longer you, now another separate person—tell the story through his or her eyes.

Pre-writing/brainstorming prompt:

Think back to a time in your early childhood when you were terribly frightened, incredibly happy, or when you remember how joyful your young life was. Close your eyes and put yourself back in that time. Think about these questions:

- Where are you? On vacation? In your home? At school? At the playground?

- What time is it? Bedtime? Early morning?

- What season was it? Winter? Spring? Summer or Fall?

- Who's there? Parents? Friends? Pets? What are their names? How old are they?

Chapter Two

- What sounds do you hear? People's voices? Other sounds?

- What do you feel or taste?

- How do you feel? Why are you feeling this way?

Drafting prompt:

Now, try to connect your feelings to an object or image, like a streak of lightning, a sweet treat of ice cream, or angry voices. Next, jot down your images and feelings (draw them if you can't find the words or don't have enough English yet to express them) as they come to you. Don't worry about spelling, punctuation, or grammar at this stage. Let the words flowing from your pen carry you to new pictures, words, and associations.

Peer conferencing/Revising Prompt:

- What was the total effect I wanted to achieve? Happiness? Terror? How well did I pull it off?

- Have I used words that evoke several of the senses?

- Does my piece reflect strong emotion? Did I say or imply that I was sad or frightened or happy?

As a grown woman, now able to share this painful memory, this graduate student was able to put her voice to something not talked about during her childhood in the 1940s—family separation and divorce—still taboo in many women's writing.

Many years ago, I volunteered to work with incarcerated male adolescents convicted of low-level marijuana possession under the racist policies called the "Rockefeller Laws" in New York State. The law, since repealed, served to fill up New York State medium-security sites where many of these youth had also left school before graduating. Many of them "tested" as a first-to-third grade level in their reading and writing on state-wide assessments, and yet, when asked, many of them had quite a bit to say.

One young man with whom I worked and call here, "M.J." was very much a loner, sitting at a back table, not talking to others. When he finally befriended me (after months of just watching me) when asked, here is his short memoir, written in despairing tones:

> Everyone always told me how dumb I am. I was born in Ohio, we left there when I was one. Left my father behind. My mother always said I'd be just like him—he was a bad man—and I never see him— and so when she moved away [his mother moved south and left M.J. when he was just in the eighth grade] I just got in lots of trouble. I'm not very smart.

M.J., indeed older than the others in this class began to recount freely to me his life in bits and pieces, saying finally, "You're the only person that ever visited me. But this time in here has really changed my life."

I like to think that through his writing and talking about his writing, M.J. had become "critical" and pensive of the world around him and his place, and voice, in it.

Finally, I share here a short piece of a memoir that my refugee student shared. (Note: It too him a full three years to trust me, recently calling me "maman" and signing his texts to me with "ton fils" —always reminding me that his life (at the age of 19): "C'est une longue histoire, maman." He only shared his life stories in bits and pieces). I present a portion of his written memoir here in its original French with my translation in the following paragraph:

> Ma grand-mere n'avait pas de choix je suis reste avec elle pendant des années. Mais, vers les 2013, la mort vien frapper a la porte de ma grand-mere et j'étais obligé d'abandonner les etudes. Étant un bon ami il est aller vole l'argent de ses parents pour me donner et c'est la bas l'aventure de ton fils commence avec force patience et détermination.

Chapter Two

My grandmother had no choice and I stayed with her for years. But, towards 2013 death began to knock on my grandmother's door and I was obliged to abandon my studies. But then, a good friend had his parents give me some money and that began the adventure of your son; one I took one with a force of determination and patience.

My "son" told me after writing this, that although he had never written it down before, he finally wanted me to let "le monde" (the world) to hear his voice.

Personal writing, indeed, can be cathartic. Much scientific research on the benefits of writing (particularly on personal writing or "writing about oneself") has shown that writing can, "improve mood disorders, help reduce symptoms among cancer patients, and improve a person's health attack' (*The New York Times*, 2015).

An article published in 2015 in the *Journal of Personality and Social Psychology* (as published in *The New York Times*, January 20, 2015) goes even further by claiming that students at Duke University who were struggling with their grades found that those who participated in writing groups and were then prompted to write their personal stories not only improved their grade point averages, but also were less likely to drop out. In the long term, students who participated in these writing groups also had fewer illnesses and visits to the student health center while improving their grade point averages.

In the next two chapters, I introduce the narrative and poetry genre; a natural progression, I believe, from personal writing, as the three genres share many features, the least of which is affording the writer the opportunity to draw upon one's own experiences, dreams, wishes; making connections, often abstractly, to their lives and to the lives of others.

CRITICAL NARRATIVE WRITING

M any cultures use narrative writing. The great Greek epic stories of the *Iliad* and the *Odyssey* provide two classic examples. Blake & Blake (2002) discuss narrative use in the Old Testament as the first part of the Christian Bible, which is based primarily on the 24 books of the Hebrew Bible, and in the New Testament, the second part of the Christian biblical canon that tells stories of Jesus within the context of the first century of Christianity.

Narrative is, in school classrooms, the "classic" reading and writing genre and is introduced even to very young children in the form of fairy tales, folk tales, and ballads, with shared "lessons" across many cultures. Indeed, caretakers in many cultures turn to reading stories to their own children as being a right of passage. Narrative texts have a character, a plot and setting, are temporally ordered and are often based on goals and/or morals. The global structure of narrative can be seen around the world through fairy tales like "Cinderella", which is written in several languages and told among various, diverse cultures around the world.

However, the narrative genre, especially in Western and Asian cultures around the world, is often seen as inferior that of the scientific/mathematical, i.e., expository and persuasive genres—genres that prepare students best to become "college- and career-ready", thereby competing with equal footing on a global stage.

But who wants to live in a world without storytellers and stories? In classrooms around the world, teachers build on the students' concept of story by first making the crucial connection between reading and writing so that students have many samples of writing across disciplines. Teachers, then, may help students examine the elements of story structure—plot, setting, character, theme, and point of view—in the books students read and then have them apply these elements in the stories they write. As readers, students think about how an author used a particular structure and consider its impact in a variety of ways; then, as writers, they can experiment with structure in the stories they write and consider the impact on those who read their stories.

Some of the best ways to get students to write "traditional" narrative include retellings, wordless books, and the use of discipline-specific books where, for example, students can turn an inanimate object (e.g., a linear equation) into a central character.

For example, in a retelling, students can retell stories (or even expository text, as we will demonstrate) orally and in writing to deepen their understandings of how authors use narrative elements and devices to develop stories. Young children and English learners (ELs), for example, can retell by using pictures—whether cut out or drawn with their own hand.

Like retellings, wordless books help writers (again especially for reluctant writers and/or inexperienced writers in English) understand the structure of narrative better as they are afforded opportunities to not only deepen their understandings, but also to show their creative side. In an undergraduate class I taught, I used the book *Carl's Christmas* (cite) to elicit retellings from our students, reminding them there was no one "correct" way to accomplish this, but to remember to focus on at least one narrative structure. Very funny drafts were penned and revised, as many of my students took on the character of Carl (the main character—a large and loving dog who takes the baby out riding on his back on Christmas Eve to see the lights and joy of the city) in unexpected and creative ways.

Using content-specific books work well in eliciting stories from all levels of writers, too (as well as aiding students' comprehension in a particular discipline). Below are some my favorite math stories:

The Greedy Triangle	Marilyn Burns
Math Curse	Jon Scieszka
How Big is a Foot?	Rolf Myller
A Remainder of One	Elinor J. Pinczes
How Much is a Million?	David M. Schwartz
Anno's Mysterious	
Multiplying Jar	Masaichiro
The Number Devil	Hans Magnus Enzensberger

Using narrative devices (such as personification used below in "Rock Cycle") is indeed one good way for students to sort out difficult content material. Here is one of my undergraduate student's final narrative piece where, as a soon-to-be Earth Science teacher, the rocks in the "Rock Cycle" have tales of their own to tell:

Rock Cycle

This is the story behind the birth and formation of three sisters—igneous, metamorphic, and sedimentary. Even with their different textures and compositions, these girls with always share a cycle. Metamorphic was the oldest child and she was the most serious of all the girls. As the oldest, she was under the constant pressure of Mother Earth to show her sisters how to behave. One day, metamorphic decided to explore her mother's bedroom that was called the Mantle. When she entered the room, she was hit with extreme heat and the weight of the air on her body transformed her smooth surface into wrinkly layers.

Sedimentary was the middle child; no one could ever predict her mood. One day she would be in a playful mood and turn into a conglomerate rock composed of smaller rocks that had been washed away by the water and compressed by pressure. Each rock was a different color or shape, a gift from Aunt River, who with her power of weathering and erosion gave her a new rock to add to her physic with every visit. Another day she was turned into shale; this was her darkest mood as she would turn pure black and glassy, reflecting the radiant energy of her father, Father Sun On a good day ,she was sandstone. Her color would turn into golden sand with beautiful layers and she would gain a layer with each year she grew older.

The youngest of them all was igneous—the day that metamorphic entered the Mantle, she accidently released magma from deep in Mother Earth's bedroom that traveled up to the surface. When this magma cooled down it turned into the smooth gray igneous rock. She is the most luxurious of the three and enjoys the finer things of life. This is why you will always see her embellished with either small (extrusive) or large (intrusive) crystals.

On Mother Earth's 1000th birthday, the girls wanted to surprise their mom with a meaningful gift. Father Sun gave Mother Earth his radiant energy and Aunt River provided her with cool water. After brainstorming for hours, the girls decided on a gift: a great big collage that displayed the creation of each girl. The collage was so accurate and beautifully made that Mother Earth gave it a special name: The Rock Cycle. To this day, scientists use it as a way to commemorate how each girl was born and created.

Maribel, a middle school English language learner, reflects a sense of excitement around finding and expressing new multiple voices through experimentation with different genres. Although heavily modeled on a Shel Silverstein poem, anyone who knew Maribel knew the following "story" (as she insisted it was) in all its playfulness, most certainly reflected her personality:

Never Kiss an Alligator

Never kiss an alligator, hug an alligator, pat, poke, push, hit, kick or even touch an alligator, because alligators bite! When you meet an alligator usually at a zoo, what should you do? Whatch, look and learn, for alligators are fasanating! Alligators are ancient and lived when the dinosaurs lived about two hundred million years ago. The name alligator is from a Spanish word "el lagarto" which means the lizard. Lizards do look like miniature alligators. Alligators are found in only two parts of the world: a few in eastern China most in the warm southeastern United States especially Louisiana and Florida. Alligators live in water beside water half in and half out of water. They stay in ponds beside an algae-covered pond in swaps, marshes, lakes, rivers, streams, and somethmes in people's swimming pools, fishponds and in water on golf courses.

And yet, how do we get students to write critical narrative? And what does it look like (considering by definition this genre is defined by narrative devices and narrative components such as character and plot)? What if students eschew these rules and want to tell tales in their own way?

One such attempt came from another incarcerated youth with whom I worked. He had just written a piece on Malcolm X, embellishing his life with storytelling features (in response to the teacher's prompt to write: "Do you feel education is the passport to the future?) when his teacher said to him, "Write this over, that's not what I asked, that's a story."

The student replied:

Why write it over? What's wrong with it? I'd rather change the question—like Malcolm X said, if you get an education, it's a *tool* for the

future. If I had the education they had (i.e., Malcolm X and his follow-
ers) I sure wouldn't be sitting here trying to write this essay.

Narrative, like the genre of personal writing we have presented earlier, and poetry which we present next, are truly the three genres of
writing that can (best) elicit emotion, memory, connection to family; to culture, while at the same time affording students the opportunities to not only a greater understanding of a topic, like through
"The Rock Cycle" above, but to the structure of the genre with
which they are working. Narrative can also help students begin to
question—and to write stories on their own terms, not bound by
rules of what narrative *should* be and *should* look like.

Again, I turn to the work of Sharma (the native of Nepal),
who through his quest of learning to write in a Western society,
learned that the power of the written word is paramount to "access"
not only oneself, but a larger world. He writes that this newfound
understanding on his part has had great and lasting "implications
of using narratives for the teaching of writing in the context of increasingly globalized classrooms" (Sharma, pg. 53).

CRITICAL POETRY WRITING

P oetry, traditionally defined, is a "division of literature; a piece of literature written in meter; verse" and/or a "compressed form of literature [that] expresses great depth of meaning" (*2018, American Heritage Dictionary*). Poetry by its very nature defies traditional definition and is perhaps best described as a genre that uses a nontraditional writing style and language.

Consider how Gordan (1993), a children's author, expresses her understanding of poetry: "Poetry is the onion of readers. It can cause tears, be peeled layer by layer, or be replanted to grow into new ideas. And it adds taste, zest, and a sharp but sweet quality that enriches our lives".

These are Blake's (1990) ideas on why we write poetry:

> Poetry is a basic way for individuals to learn enough about their culture to become a welcome member of it. Through writing poetry we tell people some thing they didn't know or hadn't put into works before. But we write poems in order to know (p.19).

And this is Martin's (1998) advice on why we need to teach poetry:

> Teaching people to write poems requires first of all that for a limited period of time they will be forced to open their eyes and ears, to take off the blinders and let the images pour in—a necessary first step toward taking life seriously and even, I suspect, a good way to start taking responsibility for themselves and for the world they can finally see (p.36).

Chapter Four

Poetry is indeed a specific genre of literature, one that includes as some of its elements the notions of rhythm and rhyme, that evokes emotions and depth of meaning, and that may help us as human beings to construct and to reconstruct our own realities. In the classroom, poetry can become an open invitation for students to respond, experience, and celebrate through language.

The expectation of writing "good" poetry in the classroom is difficult and frightening for even the best students (and teachers!). In fact, for many children, and especially for beginning readers and writers, writing traditional poetry is simply not an option. According to Koch (1970), this is because poetry itself is in the way that children write: "[A] poetic tradition . . . that demands rhyme, meter and exalted subject matter is not child-poet-friendly". Children must therefore have alternate, or nontraditional, models of poetry that speak to them where the "...language and syntax is not so far away...that he nor she couldn't get close to it in feeling and tone". Children need to feel they can express themselves in their own words and in their own voice. (Some examples of nontraditional poetry can be found today in popular culture, including rap and hip-hop music).

As teachers, we must prepare ourselves for teaching poetry, especially to beginning and/ or reluctant students. We need to understand our students' fears and give them permission to try almost anything. We need to search for lots of good models for poetry (including the silly poetry of Shel Silverstein and the clean rap poetry of Tupac just before he died). We need to let our students experiment with rhyme and rhythm, with shape and form, and most of all, with voice. It is in finding their voices that the best writing, and hence the best poetry, shines through. Indeed, Duthie & Zimit (1992) acknowledged (in their work with primary grade students) that even though poetry is the most neglected genre in our class-rooms and a genre not readily accessible to children, it is the one that helped them to become excited to read and write more while also discovering their voices.

In this chapter, I take a different approach. Here, by looking into an actual middle school classroom, where the teacher had introduced a unit on poetry, I was able to see and learn how she moved her students, successfully, through the process of writing "critical" poetry, even though these students were beginning and/or reluctant writers.

Emma's Middle School Classroom

Emma's classroom was unique. In her urban classroom, each of her fifth- and sixth-grade students had been labeled with either a behavioral or an academic learning disorder. Furthermore, at least half of her class was learning English as a Second language (ESL); all were poor, and most (according to what Emma had heard other teachers and administrators say) were considered "uneducable", as evidenced by their state assessment scores in reading and writing. (Her students' tested reading and writing abilities were solidly on a first- or second-grade level). And yet, Emma persisted. First, she insisted that all her students write. Moreover, they were motivated to write more and to write well (it is very important to note here that most standardized state exams now test for poetry. In fact, a poem has appeared every year (as of this writing) on New York State's fourth-grade and eighth-grade standardized English Language Assessment (ELA) for the last decade or so.

Chapter Four
Haiku and Diamante Poetry

Emma's unit on poetry began with a walk outside. She encouraged her students to pick up objects—sticks, rocks, snow in the win-ter— and to hold them, feel them, close their eyes and describe them, and even talk to them. Back inside, with the students seated with their objects, fresh from the physical activity and curious, she would introduce a particular form.

Next, she would model poetry that she or some other students had written, using their objects and the poetic structure of the hai-ku, for example. Haiku is probably the most familiar syllables ar-ranged in three lines of 5,7, and 5 syllables, respectively. Haiku is very precise and concise.

Finally, without little further "formal" instruction (except, of course, for the form and various sample), she would let her stu-dents write. Here are some examples.

One young student wrote the following simple haiku:

I have a snowball

It is part of nature

It snows all Winter

After instruction, this student, too, wrote diamante poems. These poems are set in a structure that is well-liked by teachers and stu-dents because it is simple and subtly introduces grammar and form. Diamante poetry is a seven-line contrast poem written in the shape of a diamond. One formula is as follows:

Line 1: One noun as the subject

Line 2: Two adjectives describing the subject

Line 3: Three participles (ending in -*ing*) telling about the subject

Line 4: Four nouns (the first two related to the subject and
the second two related to the opposite).

Line 5: Three participles (ending in -ing) telling about the
opposite

Line 6: Two adjectives describing the opposite

Line 7: One noun that is the opposite of the subject.

Below, Arnella describes her bed (and sanctuary) at home, cov-
ered with soft pillows and basket that held her favorite things:

Basket

Orange yellow

Carrying holding stuff making

Fruit candy clothes food,

Sleeping keeping using

Purple soft

Bed

After writing this poem, the student exclaimed to her teacher,
"I like to go outside and walk around because finding stuff and
writing is easy!"

Here is "David's" diamante as Emma had just finished a lesson
on soil erosion (and he had scooped up a bit of dirt while outside)
and its consequences:

Erosion

Time   Destroy

remaining   erasing   shaping

death birth collapse rebuild

heal life

Chapter Four

Students responded well to Emma's lesson on poetry that included "found" items; items that were tangible and touchable. Like the student above, this fifth-grade boy wrote a poem (though freestyle, not haiku or diamante) after returning from a walk outside:

Stick

It dropped from a tree

And fell to the ground

I found it outside

In some leaves

There it was

On the ground

Where I saw it

I picked it up

It is rough

It was alive

Now it is dead

The wind came by

And killed it

Later, however, after this student felt successful with his freestyle poem, he, too, tried his hand with diamante poetry, seemingly finding and expressing his own sense of identity through this poetic form:

Me

Restless Tired

Running Playing Hanging

Ball Book Hall Shoes

Rapping Shopping Reading

Big Bad

Me

Ball

Oval Big

Throwing Running Kicking

Football Basketball Baseball Soccer Ball

Bouncing Passing Shooting

Round Hard

Rock

As "critical" as some of these poets were in their assessment of their abilities and lives were, in the jail classroom, many students told me they could never write poetry. After sharing a lot of their favorite song lyrics, I settled on the poetic verse of the rapper/songwriter, Tupac Shakur, written just before he died. He, too, wrote about loneliness and sorrow:

Sometimes when I'm alone

I cry because I'm on my own

The tears I cry are bitter and warm

They flow with life but take no form

I cry because my heart is torn

and I find it difficult to carry on

If I had an ear to confide in

I would cry among my treasured friends

But who do you know that stops that long

To help another carry on

The world moves fast and it would rather pass you by

than to stop and see what makes you cry

It's painful and sad and sometimes I cry

and no one cares about why.

And here, in a much-altered form (so as to protect him) I present a jail kid's poem (whom he admittedly said he was heavily influenced by Tupac):

Chapter Four

Where did it all begin?
Where did it all begin?
The pain and suffering that lies within.
I lie here in closed up walls, watching paint dry
Wondering where did it all begin?

Indeed, this student became a prolific writer of poetry as he told me it helped him to think and to think about his life and his future.

Poetry is often the most underutilized genre of writing there is. Teachers are afraid of teaching it; students are afraid of writing it (and are often told they are wrong). Secondary school classrooms and the professions don't make use of it, and yet, it remains an accessible and critical tool for students' freedom, creativity, and voice as well as for helping students express their learning of content area materials in new ways. It is through poetry, I believe, they learn to unlock new potential within—one that, with hope, helps them to trust themselves to not only make their voices heard but also to be brave enough to try other forms and genres of writing.

CRITICAL EXPOSITORY WRITING

Students use expository writing in many ways throughout their lifetime, and often in their chosen profession. Researchers like Newkirk (1989) and Pappas (2006) have provided compelling evidence that children as young as kindergarteners can and do write expository text. In addition, other researchers (Donovan, 2001; Kamberelis, 1999; and Pappas, 2006) have shown that direct instruction in this particular genre helps students to link their reading and writing experiences and to help students learn to differentiate among genres.

Expository writing is used primarily to explain something, provide information, and/or provide directions on how to complete a specific task, for example. Types of expository writing include newspaper articles, assembly guide instructions, or even recipes. In contrast to the previous genres, expository writing, for the most part, *does* follow a specific format including "the hook", "topic sentences", "information", "summary", and "conclusions". To achieve this, many writers employ what are commonly known as "expository text structures" that includes: description, sequence, comparison, cause and effect, and problem and solution (see Appendix B for sample graphic organizers to potentially use with each structure). Again, each of these features may be directly taught to students as they learn to craft their own expository texts. In many cases, two or more types of expository writing are combined (think newspaper articles), often blending one genre with another. By doing this, writers learn content and, perhaps, how to make sense of difficult or confusing content through the organization and writing in the expository genre.

Within the guidelines of expository writing often follows a set of guidelines, writers can make use of expository features that include: description, sequence, comparison, compare and contrast, and problem and solution. (Please note: Many graphic organizers showing and explaining how to use these features may be found easily online).

Again, teachers and writers often find it a "stretch" to write critical expository text. But there are many samples we can share with our students that include expository exposés (such as those found in *The New York Times*, for example) where while the journalists provide information on an issue such as the war in Iraq, they also offer information that helps the reader to think critically about what he or she is reading. One beautiful example of this is a recent article (juxtaposed against a background of expository texts on the horror of war) that describes one woman's attempts at keeping art as a central way to express oneself and to see the beauty around her in a war-torn country ("Where Beauty Was Long Suppressed, Art Flowers Amid Protests: Painters, sculptors and musicians are rallying to Baghdad's protests, and the capital is overflowing with political art", *The New York Times*, 2/3/2020, "Baghdad Dispatch").

Below, I present samples from two students as they learn to work with expository text. The first sample highlights how one student in a graduate education course used the genre to help him to tease out important concepts of "force and velocity" in physics so he could explain it to others. He shared his expository writing that described the concepts with his fellow classmates (i.e., the publishing stage where students are encouraged to share their work in front of the class). In doing so, he stated that this exercise, in turn, would help his high school physics students to do the same. (The text does not contain its original supplementary author-drawn diagrams). The second example presents an original draft of an expository piece where an eighth-grade student addressed the "problems" between the U.S.A. and Iraq in 2008.

Force and Velocity in Collisions

There are many situations in life when two things make a collision. Examples of collisions include a car and a bug colliding. The outcomes of all these types of collisions depend on the physics of force, mass and velocity.

When a cue ball in a game of billiards hits its target ball, both balls experience the same force but in different directions. However, the motion of the balls change in different ways because of their initial velocity and the direction of the force on them. In this case the cue ball may come to a stop, while the colored ball moves across a table. The two balls have the same mass, so the force transfers.

In a case of a car crashing into a bug, the masses of the two objects are vastly different. A car is barely effected, while the bug is squashed. In this collision both the car and the bug are hit with an equal force. However the force has a larger effect on something small with lower mass then something large with a lot of mass.

If you were colliding with a friend in a bumper car and that friend was the same weight, you would hit each other with the same force and bounce back an equal distance. However, if you bumped into someone with less mass like your little brother, he would go zooming across the floor, while you bounce back a little bit.

In conclusion, when there is a collision between two objects an equal force will be exerted on the two objects. Thus, if they are the same mass, they will be effected equally. However, if one object is more massive, its sped and direction will be effected to a much smaller magnitude then the less massive object. This is a reason many consider SUVs to be a safer option on the road because SUVs are more massive then cars and would be less effected by a collision. Of course all automobiles come with the latest collision absorption safety features.

And:

Iraq

We are having a big problem in Iraq. The war is going crazy the reason why is because more people are coming to the war. Lots of them are dying and getting hurt really bad. The people in the war need lot of help we should help them by sending them better equipment. The people in the war need lot of help we should help by sending them better equipment. They really need it.

The reason all these stuff are happen is because there dying and if there dying little by little our war will be done. There also in danger of what happen to them. Those things that happen to them should get better. So I think Obama should get them better equipment so they can do what they have to do. So they can put a stop to this war.

The reason why this is happening is because the bad people in Iraq did not want to share there oil because bush said something to them. So now there having a war about the oil they got mad about what bush told them. So now Obama is going to put a stop to this and im going to help him. Hope you do the right thing Obama.

As teachers, we can only hope that the power of this student's words 12 years ago might be transformed today into advocacy (in the form of protest, the writing of a letter to the editor of a newspaper, and beyond) as the war continues to escalate.

Interestingly, this last example really blurs two genres: an indication that both students (and real writers) often blur genres as they feel (more) confident in experimenting with non-fiction texts.

In the next chapter on persuasive writing, I highlight the natural movement from expository to persuasive in teaching students to learn to write from the perspective and structure of persuasive writing. Again, I contend that these two genres may often naturally blend together with some simple changes in structural rules, voice, audience, and purpose. As we shift to the persuasive genre in the next, and final, chapter of this notebook, I hope this becomes more clear.

CHAPTER SIX

CRITICAL PERSUASIVE WRITING

Persuasion is a part of everyday life. We use persuasion to change people's minds, to help our students think about things more critically, and to share our opinions with groups we might not have otherwise been afforded the opportunity (think letters to the editors of newspapers).

We can teach the use of persuasion by using models that highlight not only the three major ways to persuade through writing, but also by using the structure of each of these appeals. Persuasive writing centers on an argument that, like a story, has a beginning, middle, and end. Purpose and audience are crucial to this basic structure. However, it is in these three ways to persuade that writers learn to express their voices as they become more confident and, hopefully, more critical in this world.

First, writers persuade by appealing to reason using cause and effect, e.g., if we don't stop global warming, we will lose our planet; by appealing to character, e.g., to a trusted senator on why one needs to combat racism, and through an emotional appeal (often in conjunction with the first two), e.g., a writer shows her deep concern for the well-being of others and the rights of others. All three of these types of appeal are used in and out of the classroom.

Below, you will find student persuasive samples. The first sample comes from a seventh-grade student in a New York City social studies classroom. Directed to use the structure/s of writing persuasively, students were asked to write on an important topic affecting the entire world (and based on what they had studied so far in their social studies class). And yet, before this student began her piece, she felt it necessary to organize her thoughts and arguments through the use of a semantic web with "Help Stop Global Warming" as the central circle and each appeal such as, "It effects everyone and everything" in numerous circles surrounding the central circle. (See Appendix B for a scanned, original copy of this graphic organizer).

Help Stop Global Warming!

Global warming is a very serious problem that effects everyone and everything! If global warming continues it could put the whole world in danger. What global warming does is it starts to make everything go out of whack. It's created by different kinds of polutions like air pollution. Greenhouse gases also add to the global warming problem.

Global warming could end the world, the polar ice caps could melt and start a flood. Or the winter days will get hotter or it could start snowing in the summer. If it continues everything we fought for in the past wouldn't matter if there wasn't any future, like when woman's rights were fought for, what the Civil War was started for, or anything else that helped to make our present time better. Global warming isn't stopped then the future won't happen.

If global warming continues the kids of today won't have a future to look forward to. Everyone could do something to stop this from happening. No matter how little or old a person is they could still help out. People could help plant more trees, on Earth day we could copy what the French do and not use cars or buses that day or just turn off lights when were not in a room. It really doesn't matter what we do as long as we do something to help the Earth and make sure the future happens. So please help out the kids of today and the children, *Mr. President*.

Notice that not only does the student here use each of the three major ways to persuade (reason, character, and emotion), as in her words, to help the President understand the perspective of a seventh-grader. But, perhaps, too, because the President is considered a trusted audience, the student assumed that using all three appeals would strengthen her case. But, most poignantly is the topic the student chose to write about after having only been given the prompt, "persuade someone important about a crisis facing our world today", showing, indeed, that students as young as a seventh-grader are capable of and know how to write about critical social issues affecting us all.

In the next persuasive piece, a graduate student in education who currently is a teacher in a local elementary school (where her class typically holds 34 students) takes a stance (resting largely on the "reason" appeal) on what is in the best interests of her students vis à vis starting time for the school day.

Alarm Clock Blues

Dear Principal XYZ:

As you well know, the current circumstances for school start times range between 7:50–8:15 AM. This may seem like the only option, but it is not in the child's best interest. Adjusting the start time of school to 9 AM instead of 8 AM will not only increase productivity for the students but for the educators as well. Starting school later ensures the students receive more sleep and have more time to eat a well-balanced breakfast which will help positively impact the child's focus and understanding. This extra time at home also reinforces a solid family structure.

According to NPR's Sleepless No More in Seattle, students who started the day later were better behaved, better concentration, and happier with more sleep. The school changes range between 8:45–9:15 am start times. When students begin later it allows students to be fully awake when arriving at school. They also reported feeling more energized. This is also true for educators as well. Having extra preparation time in the morning will not only relieve stress but improve sleep and motivation within the work community. Students will still have the same 6½ to 7 hour day; it would just extend slightly longer. Students would be able to arrive early, if need be, to the morning drop-off, which we already have in works. The academic hours would extend from 9 am to 3:30/4 pm. While the day may be longer, it is also more convenient for families to arrange to get their child considering most workdays only go until about 5 pm in the corporate world.

However, speaking of convenience, I can see the issues one may face. Starting school at its' earlier time is easier for working parents. Those who cannot afford childcare in the early hours may need to drop the kids off first thing. This might make sending their child to school a bit more difficult, but in the long run, isn't the child's well-being what we, as a community, should focus on? Later start times will help so many children and teachers. Thank you for your consideration.

Here, the graduate student, makes her case by generally using "reason"—that is, a case based upon and backed up with fact. Using "reason" turns this piece into a straightforward case for what she is trying to persuade the audience to do.

Next, here is an example of a graduate student's plea for teaching all students the art and importance of learning to write in cursive:

Forgetting Our Roots

Over the past several decades the world has changed dramatically. Technologies such as computers, cellphones, and internet have upended our way of life. While these technologies have brought us connectivity and productivity, there have been many casualties in the technologies wake. While e-commerce has brought the downfall of behemeths such as Blockbuster as well as the proclivity of Brick and Mortar stores, that is not what I want to talk about today. I want to discuss how these technological changes have led to changes rooted in our deep cultural heritage. An example of such a change is the elimination of cursive writing instruction to our children and future generations.

Cursive writing has been considered a critical skill to be taught to our youngsters throughout the 20th Century. While pupils would first learn to write in print, they progress to learning to write cursive. Cursive writing has many advantages including a faster pace of writing then in the print form. Even the signatures that adults use in signing important forms and receipts is often written in cursive.

Many schools have begun to eliminate the instruction of cursive writing. Sadly, these children will grow in a world without a skill that was critical for their fore fathers. Instruction is taking away from them a chance to further develop their fine-motor skills as well. What will they replace teaching cursive with? What could be more important teaching them in the third grade?

While students can transition to typing, technology is not always available or can run out of batteries. Having developed writing skills is an important part of one's education. If suddenly robots were developed to do the jobs for people, would that mean that people don't need an education? Even though the use of typing in computers allows great utility for its users, typing should be considered a supplemental method of expressing writing rather then a replacement. We need to make sure we don't stop teaching essential skills to future generations.

Again, we see the use of a combination of persuasive appeals to make his case, lending weight to the belief that while expository is written without emotion, one makes the leap, as it were, into persuasive writing, usually by adding an emotional appeal to the writing.

Writers often find that they are able to move into persuasion from exposition naturally and without (often) the explicit instruction needed in each of the other genres, even if many teachers complain that learning persuasive writing takes longer and more student ability than any other genre and that for students to be, career and college ready, as represented by the state exams they must take, explicit instruction, such as the nature of the very specific three types of appeal, *is* necessary.

Finally, below is a compelling persuasive piece written by an eighth-grader in New York City, after being prompted, "Write to someone important about a major concern in today's society".

Racism

Dear Senator:

Racism is a major problem in this country. I think a law should be passed to restrict racism and get cops to arrest anyone who is being racious. Still, this might not fix the problem so there are alternatives.

One thing that should be done is to teach young kids from an early age why racism is bad and what should be done to help get rid of it. This will end up stopping racism dramaticly.

Another useful tactic to stop racism would be to show how each of us are different and unique but it should be known as a amazing thing, not a bad thing. This might help people chance or have a change of heart.

Making shows or programs on people uniting and coming together regardless of race might help those confused if it's okay to do or not. If this program could go national, it will greatly help in encouraging a non-racist society.

Helping people who are already racists might help also. I suggest asking them why they are racious and how they feel about it. Next, show them something that shows how racism affects all of us not just one person.

I conclude by saying I think racism is one of if not the worst problem in the country. It's also a major problem around the world as well. I hope, somehow, racism will be abolished in the near future. Sincerely,

CRITICAL READER RESPONSE

This chapter focuses on "student" critical response. Here, I turn to a previous article I wrote several years ago entitled, "Critical reader response in an urban classroom: Creating cultural texts to engage diverse readers", from which I will recapture and repurpose some of the salient points, prompts, and examples to highlight what I believe is another important dimension of "writing critically".

As a theoretical perspective, reader-response criticism has not adequately addressed either the role of the author and the author's social and cultural influences or the relationship between literary and other cultural texts. As instructional practices, response-oriented approaches often fail to encompass the social complexity of classroom communities with students of varying backgrounds, abilities, and experiences and the possibilities for critical inquiry into literacy practices themselves. (Rogers & Soter, 1997, p. 1)

Ebony, a young African-American girl, spoke to me often about the literature she was reading in her urban middle-school classroom. Why is it, she wanted to know, that "everything I read is about White people and boys?" Why, is it then, she added, that reading is "so-oooo boring"?

Ebony's responses to what she was reading were typical among the urban middle and secondary students I have taught and worked with over my professional career. Mostly English language learners (ELLs), often of color, labeled "special needs", and usually poor, these students held a common perspective toward the value of literature: There was no sense bothering to respond—to "talk"—to this literature because it did not, and could not, "talk" to them.

Rosenblatt's (1978) transactional theory of reader response, which describes a "poem" that exists in the mind of the reader and a text that the reader is "transacting" with, has for years successfully provided a useful theoretical direction for the literature classroom (Beach & Freedman, 1992; Blake, 1996; Martin & Leather, 1994). As students learned that there was no one "true" meaning, they were encouraged to bring their own interpretations to a discussion of text. In addition, students were afforded opportunities to resist imposed interpretations while understanding, theoretically, that all interpretations were valid.

However, later research pointed to the fact that educators had failed to attend to the responses of all students (most not having ever been formally or informally been shown how to do this) and in not doing so, have not made their "English classrooms …spaces of community for nonmainstream and oppositional students" (Hines, 1997, p. 117). As our pubic school classrooms become increasingly diverse even in the midst of populist reform that includes closing borders, and hence opportunities, to many of these students, the value of using traditional response procedures with culturally and linguistically different students needs to be, once again, carefully scrutinized, questioned, and challenged.

My concerns over the future success of reader response theories and practice within these classrooms center around their ability to "speak to" and "to let speak" the students whose varied identities are constructed within and by their cultures, ethnicities, genders, sexual orientations, races, classes, and positions in a global world. Theoretically, reader response should allow all students to "speak" and yet in practice, they do not. Further exacerbating the silencing of students, the *idea* of even teaching reader response has fallen into such disfavor that most states in the U.S. no longer deem it necessary to put it alongside other required learning standards, as it simply does not fit with the all-powerful mantra of "college- and career-ready".

Rosenblatt's(1978) challenge to a text-centered (i.e., new critical) approach that renders the reader "invisible" continues to be important. Nevertheless, it is crucial to extend Rosenblatt's transactional approach to make the "silenced" reader visible. This is what I call a "critical" response model—a model that helps the teacher encourage silenced readers to generate their own text so that they can engage with text more interesting that the traditional canon and thus become more willing and able to respond.

A critical model of reader response to literature is based primarily on the notion that through a certain ideology or stance, one can look "critically" at the assumptions and perspectives of a text or an author around, for example, gender, race, class, sexual orientation, immigrant or refugee status, and one's place in the larger world. (Please see Appendix C for a table that delineates the major tenets of each type of response I write about here; noting that although I have not discussed a "moral" response, I do include it for comparative purposes). These ideologies and stances are grounded in critical, feminist, postcolonial and other theoretical frameworks that:

> Highlight the role of culture and cultural identity in both writing and reading, the relationship of literary texts to other cultural texts, and the ways in which interpretive communities may be sites of cultural reflection and struggle as well as textual interpretation. (Soter, et al., 1996, p.1)

This "extended" reader response theory says that the author's stance and the reader's stance both affect the "poem" that is created in the reading transaction. In practice, then, it makes sense to begin with texts and authors whose ideological stances are familiar and appealing to readers. In urban classrooms where many students have had little exposure to literary texts that connect to their lives, it makes sense to begin with the students' own texts. These are what I call "cultural texts"; texts that reflect the students' own ideologies and stances.

A critical model requires, at least in its initial stages, texts that students are willing to engage with—recall Ebony's comments about "White people and boys". A critical model of reader response theory not only provides an alternative framework from which students can respond to literature (outside of what Beach, [1994a, 1994b] calls the "traditional, White male privilege" stance) but also affords opportunities for students to create the literature of the classroom. These student-generated "cultural texts" become the vehicle for critical response.

What is a Cultural Text?

When one composes a text, one composes a social self (Bakhtin, 1981, 1986; Dyson, 1992; 1993). As students write, they weave stories of their lives and experiences, shaping their texts as they shape their identities. According to Bakhtin, the act of composing a text is always an act of "dialogism". That is, when a writer uses words, she "necessarily engages or responds to past and present discourses", so that each word "smells of the context and contexts in which it has lived its intense social life" (Ewald, 1993, p. 332).

A cultural text, then, is a text that "smells" of context, experience, of reality. In the twenty-first-century classroom or in the makeshift classrooms among refugees in Paris, it is a text that releases scents of gender, race, class, linguistic heritage, country of origin, immigrant status, and community; a text that reflects the particular aspirations, struggles, and realities of the learners themselves. Cultural texts are the "stuff" of students' lives, created and responded to in ways the incorporate the semiotics of a culture (Blake, 1995a). Cultural texts are inherently "dialogic" and "answerable" (Bakhtin, 1991, 986) as multiples voices in any classroom conflict and collide in response to one another. Creating one's own text can be "personally transforming" (Rogers, 1997, p. 102) as students' writings help them to connect their lives to other texts in the social world.

The rest of this chapter presents samples of some of the texts that urban students in a middle-school classroom created and also responded to in beginning, or potentially, critical ways. The texts and the responses to the texts illustrate four major, interrelated points. First, responses may encourage students' "desire to understand and feel empathy for different people, times, and dilemmas" (Enciso, 1994, p. 524). Second, responses may help students to learn to use their own cultural resources to make connections not only with a text, but with themselves and to others. Third, responses to other students' writing can help students to learn to "raise challenges to stereotyped interpretations of characters" (Enciso, 1994, p.527) as they move away from the strict interpretations and explanations based on the assumptions of the dominant culture. Finally, and perhaps most importantly, as students attempt to articulate "critical" responses to their own texts, these responses help prepare them to become critical of other texts and to learn to challenge the pervading discourses of racism and sexism that pervade their own and society's cultural stances and beliefs.

Ebony and her peers spent a lot of time writing in their response journals about what they were reading. Because their teacher had modeled many types of response, his students were, in theory, "free" to react to the text in ways they felt appropriate, understanding that there could, indeed, be more than one interpretation of what they were reading.

Most of these students, however, seemed to understand response to mean either writing a summary of what they had read or simply telling their teacher whether or not they liked the book. Nayda, a native Spanish speaker, made many entries like this one in her journal:

> Today I am reading another book called The President in American History. This is a very good book to me. It's better than the book I read before And It's called The war of 1812. And it's boring. But I think the book that I'm reading now is better than I read before. Well, I'll see you later.

And Laura, like Nayda, a native speaker of Spanish, wrote this about the novel, *Her Seven Brothers* (1993).

> Dear Teacher: What can I tell you I am just in the 3rd page. I just don't get it that it says she has Brothers, but she doesn't!

And the next day:

> I think I don't like this book anymore I think I am getting board of it so I am just going to read my favorite page.

Unfortunately, most of these young students simply found the books they were reading too hard or too boring and their responses reflected those realities (See Blake, 1995b)

Yet, the students were not just responding in these ways because they found the trade books they were reading too difficult. They were responding as they were because the texts they were reading were not connected to them, nor did they help them to feel a connection to someone or some place in any way. The students were unable and unwilling to relate to the text. A factual account of the war of 1812, although it certainly dealt with a momentous occasion in American history, simply did not connect (perhaps by virtue of the way it was written) with the social and cultural contexts of poor urban life—a life that is the reality for these students, and they are acutely aware of this fact.

The teacher, too, was acutely aware that his students were making what he called "standard reader responses" to the texts of the classroom, despite his modeling and teaching of a variety of response techniques. It was not until students began to create and engage willingly with their own texts that he understood that student-generated texts could serve as initial sites for response that were much more authentic and connected to the students' lives. As in the secondary English classroom Rogers (1997) studied, it was not "until the texts of the classroom were traced out into the world" that this teacher felt he was truly hearing students respond in personal, authentic, and often deeply profound ways.

For example, during a writers' workshop, Jahaira, another native Spanish speaker, wrote a story about learning to be both cool and tough. Entitled "Sugar and Spice" and read during Author's Chair (see esp. Graves & Hansen, 1983, for a wonderful rationale and samples of "Author's Chair"), this piece prompted many responses, both orally and in writing from her peers. An excerpt appears below:

Once upon a time there were two girls. Their names were Joan and Joanna. Their nick names were Sugar (Joan) Spice (Joanna). Joan was real sweet, but Joan-na was always in the streets playing with real little shorts. One day there were in school and Joanna and her friends were laughing at Joan because she didn't dress cool. Joan said, "Shut up!" A girl named Maria came and said, "Who are you talking to!" Joan said, "to all of you!" Maria said, "Well I guess I have to fix this mess!" Maria slapped Joan. They started punching each other and pulling hair. The principal came and stoped them. Maria said, "I am not finished with you Joan!"...

The principal gave both of them a detention.... Then they started cursing each other....The detention teacher, Mrs.Rivera came and said...Now be nice...but she didn't know how to talk English... so the principal gave them a 2 day suspension. Joan was at her house and her friend Jennifer came. and told her that she was going to make her cool. She got Joan's bangs out, washed her hair, blow dried it, put contact lence on her, gave her cool clothes, put lipstick, eyeliner and blush on her. Then when the suspension was over, she went to school and everybody's mouth opened, even the teachers. Everybody said, "Wow Joan!" She said, "Don't call me Joan call me Sugar Baby!" When she went on the playground even Joanna's mouth opened. Then Maria came and said... "Stupid." Joan kicked Maria in the mouth so hard that she flew and she never messed with her again. Joan and Joanna talked it over and said, "Let's be ordinary like all these kids that are hearing this story [who are]not cool!" They were ordinary for all of there lives. And nobody messed with them again.

Jahaira understood that being cool and tough were qualities considered absolutely essential to fit in and to "survive" in the world. And yet she also knew that being cool was a liability. Her classmates knew these things, too. The girls in particular struggled with the contradiction as they tried to establish their identities in this urban environment. Most of the students reacted and responded to this piece in enthusiastic and even critical ways. For example, in response to Mr.Rassel's suggestion that his students write about the ending, a particular character, or even why or how someone becomes cool, they wrote, in part:

They wanted to be ordinary because they didn't want to have any problem being cool.

Joanna was cool because she was always in the streets talking with everybody. And Joan was all-ways doing homework. The principal is always everywhere watching every-body. Everybody hated her!

In these response journal entries, students did not write that they were bored or didn't understand the storyline. Instead, they wrote about being "ordinary", how being in the streets "talking" made one cool, and about why the principal is so hated. (Interestingly, they did not comment on Mrs. Rivera's inability to speak English—perhaps because it was so common and familiar that they didn't even think to mention it). Like many other students in their class, they responded by drawing on their own experiences, thereby validating the significance of the events in the story and providing opportunities for further discussion and the potential for critical response. And these opportunities for critical response did come.

Shortly after "Sugar and Spice" had been shared, I met with the girls for our regular writers' group. When I asked them to talk about the issues raised in the story, the girls responded excitedly to the inherent conflict in being cool, being smart, and staying out of trouble.

Asha offered detailed suggestions on how I might dress to look cool (go buy a black and purple dress, get black earrings and those black things that go over the eyes—ya look good, you get the mens around you!).

Tamika responded thoughtfully to the question I posed, "So how come we just don't walk away and not fight?":

Tamika: I don't fight. I'm a sweet angel—only one time this girl in my after-school program, they just bug me so much, they be getting me nervous... and she got me mad, and I got her eye. I didn't mean to hurt her, and I got mad, I dunno, I just can't help it. I don't know why.

Being cool and tough was a recurring theme in the students' writing and in the ways they responded. As in the story, "Sugar and Spice", the girls understood that kids who did their homework weren't cool—one simply could not be cool and smart at the same time.

The boys, too, had a lot to say and write about in response to the piece, "Sugar and Spice." In fact, two of the more quiet boys in the class responded to the issue of being cool and tough by writing a play entitled, "Homey is Back".

Boys: (two Boys walk to the store) (Boys see a big box and get closer)

Homey: (pop's out of the box)

1st boy: Look, it is a man drest as a clown. 2nd boy: Look it is a clown name Homey. Homey: do you want candy boys Boys:(are so smart they say NO!) Boys: Our mom's tell us Not to take candy from strangers and some Man put poysen in candy Homey: Your mom's dont make sence and they are so old they are past 38 year old that's why your mom's are so old and Now come on let's go to the alley! 1st boy:Why do you want us to go the alliy Homey: I have some goodes for you boy's in my van 1st boy:Come on then Homey, the clown Let's Go to you van.

(When Boys get to the alley Homey push's [them] in the van)

Homey: My partner Cookie drives the van-Step on it now. (they left they went 80 miles a hour they left to canada to sell the boys. Homey sells 1st boy 1st and then 2nd boy)

Boys are big and all ready went to college) Boys are men now when the Boys go to Bed they get sad because they cannot see their parents in Canada. When they get older they look for Homey and buy a car when they buy the car Boy's go to Chicago and try to find Homey)

Boy's find Homey's partner cookie and boy's take him to a big room)

lst boy: Take's his gun and tells cookie find Homey and tell me where he is

Cookie: (did not say anything)

1st boy: (hit cookie with the gun) Boy's did not know that Homey was't in Chicago he was in Washington, selling other kids. Boy's go to Washington and look for Homey and Boy's kill cookie. Boys want to kill Honey too...and when they got to the whitehous they see Homey in the corner...) 2nd boy: Get him now!(Boys run as fast as they could) Homey runs to the stars of the white house, 2nd boy shot Homey in the Back with his gun) 1st boy: Homey your body is lain there (laughing). He said the end of Homey. Homey is finish the world now can live in peace the End of Homey.

The play, when read aloud and shared in author's chair, prompted even more discussions of, and critiques of, the urban violence around them. Students wrote and talked about the realities of their lives—poison in candy, not being able to talk to strangers, guns, and gang violence. Interestingly, most of the students were able to justify the boys' killing of Cookie and Honey in order to obtain "world peace". These issues were the "stuff"of their lives, and it was around these issues that response and potential for response was happening in this classroom.

Chapter Seven
Cultural Texts and Cultural Identities

These students have shown us (through examples of how they created their own cultural texts and responded to them in potentially critical ways) how an extended theory of reader response can support effective teaching practices among diverse populations. Simply put, these urban, diverse students began to "spontaneously extend... the ways in which social issues are related to literacy practices"(Rogers, 1997, p.109) as they used the techniques of critical reader response to make crucial connections between texts and their own lives. For example, writing and responding critically about the seemingly contradictory nature of being "cool"and "tough" in the piece, "Sugar and Spice", not only provoked a number of empathetic responses but also gave students opportunities to offer "solutions", solutions that were not at all "mainstream". In the play, "Homey is Back", the authors, through the characters themselves, challenged stereotyped representations of urban boys and their reasons for violence, justifying the characters' killing of Homey and Cookie by a vision of "world peace", a peace, perhaps, far from the actual violent world they knew. In both cases, the students used their own cultural resources as viable experiences from which to write and respond. Because our ways of reading, writing, and responding to texts are always "inherently linked to our ways of seeing society", our current reader response approaches to texts need to be "examined for the ways in which they explicitly and/or tacitly promote particular conceptions of the world" (Hines, 1997, p.118). So-called mainstream conceptions of the world are woven through the texts our students are required to read and write about. The diverse learners in this classroom could not connect with the initial trade texts they were required to read, and therefore did not find them meaningful. And yet, when given the opportunity to create and respond to their own texts, the students became engaged.

Rosenblatt's "transactional" theory of reader response is, I believe, necessary but not sufficient when one is attempting to engage students such as those in Mr. Rassel's classroom. An extended, "critical" theory of reader response provides a viable, alternative approach for the diverse, urban classroom. It encourages all students to read and respond to literature, it accounts for the experiences and identities of diverse students, and it acknowledges and connects their experiences with social justice issues such as violence and racism. Rather than continuing to transmit mainstream culture—and the expectations and assumptions of the dominant culture—through the literature we share with our students, we educators need to help them critique and transform culture through their own texts and eventually, we hope, through a serious study of other meaningful literature. In this way, we not only acknowledge the crucial interpretations all readers bring to text, but we also help them learn to make meaningful, critical connections between the text and their own cultural identities as diverse readers.

TEACHER CRITICAL RESPONSE

In this final chapter of this book, I reproduce some of my late father's work, Robert W. Blake, Professor Emeritus, on using critical reader response in the classroom from a *teacher's* perspective, again including prompts and examples to show how the teacher can learn to teach reader response from a critical perspective. It is hoped that both the previous chapter and this one lend even more light onto the critical nature of writing and responding to reading through writing in many diverse contexts.

Here, I would like to identify what I believe to be effective, practical activities that I found useful in helping pre-service teachers (i.e., taking graduate classes to obtain a teaching license—hence they are both "teachers" and "students" at the same time) to learn to apply the principles of reader response in their own classrooms. Specifically, in several pre-service English and ESL Methods classes I have taught, I always asked the students to create a "pre-reading" task or a "pre-response" moving toward helping our new teachers then respond "intuitively," "emotionally," "personally" and from one's memory—the "memory" response.

Chapter Eight
Activities

1. Pre-reading Response.

The purpose of this task is to compel the reader to become sensitive to a dominant mood or idea within a literary piece. For instance, with the poem,"A Spring Night," I may set a task like this:

Has there ever been a time when you thought you couldn't talk to your mother or father? Write for a few minutes about such a time.

Don't worry about spelling, punctuation, or other mechanics, and don't worry about saying something you're not quite at ease with writing. You won't be asked to show your response to your fellow students or even to me, if you don't want to.

2. Initial Response.

Give this task for students to become used to responding intuitively and without inhibitions to a piece. This is the assignment I may give for an initial response.

In a short paragraph, write out what (poem, story, novel) means essentially to you. Don't worry about what anybody else thinks it means. Also, at this time, don't worry about spelling, punctuation or other writing errors. And don't worry about getting the "right" meaning. We really want to know what you think the piece means. Write as quickly as you can about your thoughts and feelings without stopping to think about them too much.

3. Memory Response.

Here is a task I use to help students become sensitive to the "memory" response.

What memories came to mind as you read this poem (story)? Don't worry about what the recollections are, how farfetched they may seem to you at this time. Your memories are a valuable part of reading literature because they help you understand the poem. Here are some sentences to use for making a memory response.

This poem (story) reminds me of a time when…

This word, this line, this part brought back memories of…

With this task, I hope that the pre-service teachers let their reading bring them memories and associations, which in turn illuminate for them the meaning of a poem or story. I find that this task is the most powerful one for allowing teachers to relate a literary piece to their lives.

4. Feeling Response

This response is what Bleich (1978) calls the"affective response", but we have chosen the word "feeling" because it appears more easily accepted and understood by students and teachers.

Here's the task I set for students to become comfortable with relating their feelings to literary pieces:

As you read this poem (or story), how did you feel? Jot down in a few sentences what your feelings were. Here are samples of the kinds of sentences you can use to show you are writing a feeling response.

Chapter Eight

Responses

In our English and ESL Methods classes, I always try to begin with a story or a poem to which I am pretty sure new teachers will want to, and be able to, response. That is, I try to choose stirring, often emotional pieces from which we hope the pre-service teachers will express their feelings.

To illustrate how to use these response prompts, I present various pre-service teachers responses to the poem, "A Spring Night" (Beloof, 1965). The poem appears first, followed by the teachers' responses.

A Spring Night

His son meant something that he couldn't name
He had his picture in his wallet,
but never remembered taking out the wallet

for anything but cash, or an address, or a name.
He could have hated him, but didn't
even though the boy reminded him
how stuck he was because of him.
He could have loved him, too, but didn't.
When Mr. Cuff came home at night
there was reading, or sitting on the stoop till dark, watching
the dead-end street he lived on fade to dark, so they didn't talk
together much at night
Sitting as usual this April evening
watching an impassively dying sun
he became aware that hesitantly his son
was coming to him out of the evening.

They sat awhile together, then quietly
the boy asked him,"Do you really like boys?
I'd just like to know that, if you really like boys
Mr. Cuff was stunned. The sun set quietly.
Communication was a rusted hinge to Cuff.
he sought some way convincingly to say
"There's just the word I've wanted to say
but couldn't say."
"Like is the word,"thought Cuff" I'm damned, "
said Mr. Cuff under his breath.

Finally the boy shuffled off. Cuff went to bed.
"What's that you're mumbling over there in bed?"
Asked Mrs. Cuff in the dark. Cuff lay still as death.

Initial Response

Melissa: Thought this was a sad poem about a father who either couldn't and didn't want to see his son

Robbie: I liked this poem because it showed how a father feels when not able to see his son. Or didn't want to.

Kim: The poem started out sad and I expected it to wind up happy, when the way I see it, it remained sad. I really don't care for the poem. Sorry!

Katrina found the poem as being sad.

Miguel: My response to the poem is that it was dull. Cuff is a very withdrawn man he doesn't care. I think he was trying to communicate with Cuff and be a friend to him. He wanted someone to talk to.

Christof: Rather depressing but was easy to read. The the father hardly ever thought about his son. He didn't really I have any feelings for him. Eventually he realized he liked him.

Memory Response

Diane: I really didn't understand it at all. What I did understand I liked because I could relate to it with our relationship with my father. Sometimes it feels like my own Father resents me but we still get along.

Donna: During my first reading of "A Spring Night", I was reminded of my relationship with my father, the man whom I call dad is really my step-father. He married my mom and adopted me when I was seven years old yet I feel I barely know him. He never made the effort to get close to me, for which I no longer blame myself, as he is the same way with his three other daughters by his first marriage. He doesn't communicate well with his family, which I think is a major problem for Mr. Cuff. "Communication was a rusted hinge to Cuff." Not only with his son who must be very confused where his father is concerned, but also with his wife, who he refuses to confide in, despite his feelings of frustration and loneliness.

Feeling Response

Robin: After reading and pondering the poem, "A Spring Night", I couldn't help but be reminded of the classic folk song, "Cat's in the Cradle." The son relates the trials a father has in expressing his love for a child and the ambiguous feelings and attitudes heads toward his son. Eventually, the man realizes that his son is grown, and is just like him. I really felt or sensed this ambiguous ambivalent attitude that Mr. Cuff had for his son in "Spring Night". Mr. Cuff not only suffers the inability to express his emotions to his child, he also is unsure of his feelings toward his son. This is a highly tragic element of the poem, a father's lack of love for his own flesh and blood.

   Unfortunately I think this is a common attitude today and so many innocent, helpless children suffer emotional scars by feeling unloved and insecure in this troubled world. obviously, Mr. Cuff's son, young and innocent, is aware of his father's lack of emotional ties to him. How tragic and sad. Any yet I almost felt a tint of sadness for Cuff. Perhaps he, like his father before him, is incapable of loving because he has never been loved. And saddened because of the oppressive trapped feeling he has toward his child.

   It is quite clear that Mr. Cuff blames his situation and stagnant life on the birth of his child, this is highly selfish but yet also common in our world. But I sensed that Mr. Cuff saw himself in his child and he likes him. Like himself, Mr. Cuff was unable to hate or love himself and his child. The pain the boy suffers in asdeep, and hurtful as Mr. Cuff's. I also felt a sense of deep-seated emotion for the child. Mr. Cuff lay still as death after his son finalizes his belief that his father doesn't love him.

Chapter Eight

It is as if the son knowing he is unloved will reject his father and Mr. Cuff lies still as death because a living part of him has just died. Perhaps Mr. Cuff does love his son but is unable to recognize or acknowledge this emotion. The poem really created a sense of the typical dysfunctional family in today's society. The inability to love oneself and each other.

Because we had been so successful in eliciting pre-service teachers responses to "A Spring Night", I decided to try another "stirring" poem about a father with the poem, "In Those Winter Sundays" (Hayden, 1966).

Our first task was to assign a pre-reading or "pre-response" before giving the teachers the poem to read. Thus, I asked our students to think of a time they remembered about their fathers, either pleasant or unpleasant before reading and responding to the poem itself. Here is what Nordene, a pre-service ESL teacher wrote:

It is very hard to write about my dad. I can't imagine writing something critical of him or showing it to anyone else. There are times when he really gets to me, times I remember where I was little and I was very angry with him. I hated it when he tickle me because he never knew it when enough was enough. Maybe that's his greatest fault, he takes things to extremes. Discipline was extreme. Although he certainly didn't abuse us in anyway, I was afraid of him, because he never hesitated to spank. What seem to be his only way of dealing with yes behavior. I hated that. I hated that there didn't seem to be much of a gray area things were right or wrong and the reason was because he said so. Head of the house. Take it to extremes. He mellowed out, now of course. I've seen him help mom in the kitchen lately. Never, in the old days. Women's work. He had his paper to read. I hated that what I was doing was never of any consequence: "Go help your mother". But he has changed. This trip I could even disagree with him and I didn't feel afraid of getting a lump in my throat. He is still extreme. Politically, socially, ethically. I admire him for sticking to his guns but I'm not there for him to impose his opinion on any more and that his freedom. That is being grown-up. I don't think I like that feeling. In some way I'm not subordinate anymore. What a relief.

It's instructive to observe what Nordene includes in her pre-reading response about her memories of her father. What strikes us in an overwhelming way are her strong feelings toward her dad, emotions which until recently she found difficult to reveal. "It's very hard to write about my dad. I can't imagine writing something critical of him and showing it to anyone else."

Note also phrases like: "...when he really gets to me," "I was angry with him," "I was afraid of him," and the repetition of phrases with the word "hate" in them: "I hate it," "I hated that..." and "I hated that...". Also, she sums up her insight into the character of her dad as "extreme": "Maybe that's his greatest fault—he takes things to extremes." "Discipline was extreme", and "taken to the extreme."

After the first part of her response in which she repeats how she "hated" his behavior, she then moves to a realization of how their early relationship has altered. When she says, "But he has changed." She points out that, in reality, her insight into his character—and her feelings for him—have become markedly different from her perception as a child of him. He's still "extreme," but she now realizes that her change in how she feels about him are what presently she understands as "being grown up." She can "even disagree with him" and no longer needs to feel afraid of getting a "lump" in her throat. She's not there to be subordinate to her dad; she's becoming independent of him. For her, "that is freedom" and she likes the feeling of being her own person. "What a relief," she concludes.

This response reflects an achingly honest exploration by a young woman who has come to terms with her childish estimations of her dad and who now knows she is no longer dominated by him. She is in the process of becoming mature and autonomous, and in a psychologically powerful way, can examine her feelings about her dad, looking at them in a detached manner and observing how she has changed from a subordinate, dependent little girl to a thoughtful young woman.

After she had written the pre-reading response, Nordene and the rest of the class was asked to read the poem,"Those Winter Sundays", and make a short, "intuitive" response to the poem. Here is Hayden's (1966) poem followed by what she wrote:

Those Winter Sundays
Sundays too my father got up early
and put his clothes on in the blueblack cold,
then with cracked hands that ached
from labor in the weekday weather made
banked fires blaze. No one ever thanked him.
I'd wake and hear the cold splintering, breaking
When the rooms were warm, he'd call,
and slowly I would rise and dress,
fearing the chronic angers of that house.
Speaking indifferently to him,
who had driven out the cold
and polished my good shoes as well.
What did I know, what did I know
of love's austere and lonely offices?

Nordene's Response:

I wonder how Hayden can write about those days, obviously with some appreciation for what his father was doing, and yet still sound so cold. The poem is very cold—winter, blueblack cold, splintering, breaking. I wonder if the coldness between him and his father ever broke and fell away or if the respect I see in the poem is just another duty returned to his father for what his father gave him? And I wonder why devotion—is devotion love—can't drive out the cold. Why must it be severe?

How can love be chronically angry? Real love is giving, as in the poem, but also forgiving. And is the father really giving in love or is it grudging duty? I guess he could have made one of his children or his wife build the fires. And he didn't have to polish their shoes. I wish I could see the man as he goes about it and understand what's in his heart. I'm not sure the poet knows that either.

As we read carefully Nordene's first, intuitive response to the poem, we observe some striking things. For her, the poem is "cold," and she cites words from the poem, using the technique of close reading to substantiate her impression: "winter", "blueblack cold", "splintering", and "breaking". She transfers the coldness of the wintering house to the coldness of her father and moves to what the poem means to her, a contemplation of the meanings of the words "devotion" and "love". As she moves from the first stage of responding to the meanings of words to the next stage of relating the poem to her own inner life, she advances from interpreting the meaning of words to creating her own personal meaning for ideas and feelings.

As she explores her questions about why "devotion" can't drive out the cold, why devotion has to be "chronically angry" and as she defines love as "giving" and also of "forgiving", she wishes poignantly she could see the father in the poem as he warms up the "Sunday house" and polishes his children's shoes, that she "could see the man as he goes about it and understand what's in his heart."

From our reading of her initial response about her father, I now wonder if Nordene doesn't unconsciously imply that she wishes to comprehend what's in her own father's heart. But, as she states wistfully in the last sentence, "I'm not sure the poet knows that [what's in the father's heart] either." In effect, she is also ignorant of what's in her father's heart. Nordene's responses are fundamentally different from what we might expect from a traditional, new critical response. Why are Nordene's pre-reading and initial responses so important for her as a teacher? How does her understanding of her feelings and emotions translate into helping her students use reader response? And, finally, how does her understanding help students become successful in responding while at the same time helping them to perhaps understand not only themselves better, but their upbringing, their culture and its norms in a new country, as well as the expectations of parents and childen?

First, she has learned to release her emotions about her complex, changing relationship with her father from her initial reading of the poem. She allows memories to inform her understanding of the poem. Although she uses the techniques of close reading, which are ordinarily associated with traditional literary criticism, she examines the words primarily for their connotative or associative values for her—not strictly for their relation to an objective, overall meaning of the text as a text.

In a manner absolutely distinct from traditional criticism, she moves outside the text and away from the text as she makes use of the poem to discover what it reveals to her. Finally, then, rather than "finding" an anticipated, "correct" meaning, she "creates" her own individual meaning, one which makes use of feelings, connects to memories "triggered" by her reactions to the poem, and which leads her to a deep and intimate knowledge of herself and of her relationship to one of the most influential persons in her life, her father. This is what we mean by literary knowing. In the classroom, this is what is meant by a "critical reader response approach" to literature. Nordene can now model this approach to her students, as her students can not only learn to express their feelings, but to engage with them, to question traditonal roles of fathers, for example, eliciting at the same time, differing critical responses from the many, varied, often voiceless students she may teach.

Brief Conclusions

It is with hope that I have attempted to highlight in this "notebook" what a critical approach to process writing is, and why, in this century's third decade, it is time that we return to its importance in addressing, and even changing, attitudes, mindsets, expectations, and outcomes of the purposes of writing in any setting. I have attempted to share with you, my "audience", not only what a critical process approach to writing is, but how it can be used in various classrooms and in various contexts, both among "traditional" students and those who are refugees, incarcerated, English-language learners, immigrants, and beyond. I am a believer that one should have a foundational understanding of how the field evolved and where it is going (so we do not run the risk of being "a-theoretical"), as well as a working understanding of how to prompt and model writing in the hope of at least beginning to lead folks to write critically. This can open up one's eyes to the sociocultural and linguistic aspects of writing, but also to its grace, beauty, and its influence around the world in terms of power and authority.

I close with this "fieldwork reflection" from one of my graduate students who was trained in engineering but decided to change careers to become a secondary-school math teacher. She writes with a renewed understanding that even in expository and persuasive writing and the emphasis on the scientific/mathematical ways of knowing, voice is always prevalent; personal, yet powerful; waiting to be heard in many genres and through the many contexts in which writers, as students and otherwise, beg to be heard.

From my fieldwork experience on observing instruction focused on writing, I was able to experience how students engage in writing activities and learn how teachers are able to facilitate writing activities. I am a first year math teacher, teaching Precalculus, College Calculus, SAT Math, and AP Computer Science A. Before doing my fieldwork I did not think it was possible to incorporate writing into my Math Courses. However, through my fieldwork and this course I was able to learn how and why it is important to have instruction focused on writing.

From my fieldwork, it became evident why math teachers must have their students write in their math courses. As a first year teacher, I am learning different teaching styles and tactics to implement for each class and each student I have. I teach in a public school in Queens, NY and my students are highly intelligent when it comes to solving mathematical equations and deriving an equation to find its derivative. However, when I ask the words, "explain" or "why" my students are unable to fully answer or explain their thinking.

From my observations it showed how instruction focused on writing can develop students' learning abilities and even their voices as they learn to express themselves in different, non-traditional ways. Writing in the classroom helps students with internalizing the characteristics of effective communication. Students are able to build the relationship between language and mathematical learning. They show evidence of logical conclusions and justification of answers and processes. Writing allows students to use facts to explain their thinking. I have also noticed that students are able to learn more when they answer a short response as opposed to multiple choice questions.

Overall, from my fieldwork experience, I have learned instruction focused on writing allows students to express new knowledge and skills in their own words. They are able to organize their ideas about a topic and share their own thoughts on a topic instead of just solving a math problem using a step-by-step process. Writing allows students to express their thinking and give students a creative aspect in mathematics. Math can be a dull subject for some students because it involves a very clear cut way to solve mathematics problems, however, writing will allow students to have different explanations and pathways to correct solutions and eventually results in all students getting the same answer. To conclude, I will continue to encourage my students to explain their thinking process and use their voices always when writing in my classroom.

APPENDIX

PEER CONFERENCING GUIDELINES

NAME: _____ DATE: _____

I read_____'s

work entitled_____

1. This is what I thought your _____(genre)_____was about.

2. This is what I liked about your piece. I especially liked this part…

3. Here's what confused me about your piece…

4. This is what you might do to make that section(s) clearer…

5. I found your piece engaging/entertaining/interesting/exciting because…

6. Your piece could be more engaging/entertaining/interesting/exciting if you were to…

7. Here are some other things (spelling, grammar) you may want to work on…

8. My overall impression of your piece and your writing style is…

Appendix

Graphic Organizer

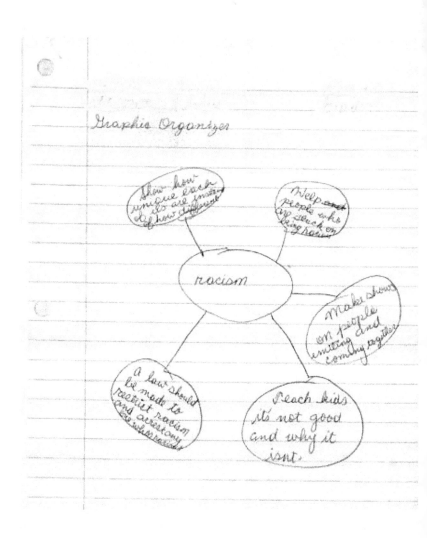

Iraq

What?
- The war is going crazy
- lots of people are dieing
- The people in the war need help

How?
- because there dieing
- There indanger
- alot of them are really hurt
- Some are pusting

Iraq

Why?
- because there flighting for oil
- because the bad guys dont want to share oil
- They wanted all for them self

"wrap up"

↳

next page

Appendix

Reader response approach in language teacher education:
Theoretical bases and applications of critical and moral response

Types of Response

TRADITIONAL

1. The teacher emphasizes the text primarily
2. The teacher guides the student to find the "correct meaning within the text.
3. The teacher directs the student to answer specific comprehension questions about elements of a literary text, such as setting, plot, characters, and theme.
4. The traditional method is essentially objective, detached, inductive, and "scientific." Emotions and personal opinions are not emphasized.
5. The student usually shares response with the teacher only.

READER RESPONSE

1. Although a worthwhile text is a necessary element, the primary emphasis is on the student's oral or written response to that text
2. The student creates her own personal meaning for the text, with the sophisticated help of an especially trained and sympathetic teacher.
3. The student gives an initial response to a literary place and then uses her/his knowledge about literary elements to support own interpretation.
4. Feelings, memories, associations, and intuition (perceptions arrived at without rational thought) are not only allowed but form the core of the reader response.
5. The student shares her responses with other children in small groups and with the whole class, including the teacher, within a learning community. Each student thus sees her individual response grown, becoming enriched and validated by the responses from her peers and teacher.

MORAL

1. An ethic of justice is based upon the idea of equality—that everyone should be treated the same.
2. An ethic of caring rests on the concept of nonviolence—that no one should be hurt.
3. While the ethic of justice has traditionally been associated with males and the ethic of caring with females, a more complex and satisfying idea of morality would include both viewpoints.
4. Readers, recognizing this dual nature of morality, may come to realize that a judgment by a character in a literary work can be interpreted according to the context in which the dilemma is framed.

CRITICAL

1. Critical response is an ideological orientation associated with gender, class, race, religion, identity, and other positionalities.
2. A critical response is a culturally relevant, ideological discourse that,
3. Assumes students' texts are artifacts of an oppressive society, and that, therefore,
4. Critical response is one powerful way to shape dominant discourses and ideologies as it challenges dominant discourses and ideologies.

REFERENCES

Atwell, N. (1987). *In the middle: Writing, reading, and learning with adolescents*. Portsmouth, NH: Heinemann.

Ayers, W. (1993). *To teach: The journey of a teacher*. New York: Teachers College Press.

Bakhtin, M. (1986). *Speech genres and other late essays*. Austin: University of Texas Press.

Bakhtin, M. (1981). *The dialogic imagination*. Austin: University of Texas Press.

Bigelow, W. (1990). Inside the classroom: Social vision and critical pedagogy. *Teachers College Record*. 91: 437-448.

Blake, B. & Maslak, M.A. (2019). *Teaching writing for all: Process, genres, and activities:* San Diego, CA: Cognella Publishing.

Blake, B.E. (2004). *A culture of refusal: The lives and literacies of out-of-school adolescents.* New York: Peter Lang Publishing.

Blake, R.W. & Blake, B.E. (2002). *Becoming a teacher: Using narrative as a reflective process.* New York: Peter Lang.

Blake, B.E. (1997). *She say, he say: Urban girls write their lives.* Albany, NY: State University of New York Press.

Calkins, L. M. (1986). *The art of teaching writing.* Portsmouth, NH: Heinemann.

Calkins, L. M. (1983). *Lessons from a child.* Portsmouth, NH: Heinemann.

Duthie, C. and Zimet. E., (1992). "Poetry is Like Directions for Your Imagination!" *The Reading Teacher* 46.1 (September 1992): 14-24.

Dyson, A. H. (1993). *Social worlds of children learning to write in an urban primary school.* New York: Teachers College Press.

Elbow P. (1981) "One to One Faculty Development." In: Noonan, J. (Ed). *Learning About Teaching: New Directions for Teaching and Learning.* Jossey-Bass.

Gilbert, P. & Taylor, S. (1991). *Fashioning the feminine: Girls, popular culture, and schooling.* North Sydney, Australia: Allen & Unwin.

Graves, D. H. (1983). *Writing: Teachers and children at work.* Portsmouth, NH: Heinemann.

Kincheloe, J. In Agnello, M.F. & Reynolds, W. M. (2016). *Practicing critical pedagogy: The influences of Joe L. Kincheloe.* (p.124). Springer Press.

Kell, C. (1997). "Literacy practices in an informal settlement." In Prinsloo, M. and Breir, M. (Eds.), *The social uses of literacy: Theory and practice in South Africa* (pp. 235-256). Philadelphia, PA: John Benjamins Press.

Koch, K. (1970). *Wishes, lies, & dreams.* New York: Chelsea House Publishers.

Lensmire, T. J. (1994). *When children write: Critical re-visions of the writing workshop.* New York: Teachers College Press.

Lensmire, T. J. (1993). Following the child, socio-analysis, and threats to the community: Teacher response to children's texts. *Curriculum Inquiry*, 23: 265-299.

Martin, V. (1988, February 7). Waiting for the story to start. *The New York Times Book Review*, pp. 1, 36.

Murray, D. (1968) *A writer teaches writing: A practical method of teaching composition.* Boston: Houghton Mifflin.

References

Pappas, C.C. (2006). The information book genres: Its role in integrated science literacy research and practice. *Reading Research Quarterly*, 41: 22-25.

Sharma, G. "Cultural Schemas and Pedagogical Uses of Literacy Narratives." In Blake, B.E. & Maslak, M.B. (2019) *Teaching writing for all: Process, genres, and activities.* San Diego: Cognella Publishing.

Willinsky, J. (1990). *The new literacy: Redefining reading and writing in the schools.* New York: Routledge.

CPSIA information can be obtained
at www.ICGtesting.com
Printed in the USA
LVHW011138060221
678443LV00008B/262